Resting in the Finished Works of Jesus

Stay Seated in Your Executive Authority

Pastor James T. Elam Jr.

WESTBOW
PRESS®
A DIVISION OF THOMAS NELSON
& ZONDERVAN

WestBow Press books may be ordered through booksellers or by contacting:

WestBow Press
A Division of Thomas Nelson & Zondervan
1663 Liberty Drive
Bloomington, IN 47403
www.westbowpress.com
1 (866) 928-1240

Because of the dynamic nature of the Internet, any web addresses or links contained in this book may have changed since publication and may no longer be valid. The views expressed in this work are solely those of the author and do not necessarily reflect the views of the publisher, and the publisher hereby disclaims any responsibility for them.

Scripture taken from the King James Version of the Bible.

Scripture taken from the Amplified Bible, Copyright © 1954, 1958, 1962, 1964, 1965, 1987 by The Lockman Foundation. Used with permission.

Scripture quotations taken from the Amplified® Bible (AMPC),
Copyright © 1954, 1958, 1962, 1964, 1965, 1987 by The Lockman Foundation
Used by permission. www.Lockman.org

Scripture taken from The Message. Copyright © 1993, 1994, 1995, 1996, 2000, 2001, 2002. Used by permission of NavPress Publishing Group.

Scripture quotations marked (NLT) are taken from the Holy Bible, New Living Translation, copyright © 1996, 2004, 2007 by Tyndale House Foundation. Used by permission of Tyndale House Publishers, Inc., Carol Stream, Illinois 60188. All rights reserved.

The Bible translated from the original text and paraphrased in contemporary speech with commentary. Copyright © 2014 by Francois du Toit. All rights reserved. Scripture taken from THE MIRROR. Copyright © 2014. Used by permission of The Author.

Any people depicted in stock imagery provided by Getty Images are models, and such images are being used for illustrative purposes only. Certain stock imagery © Getty Images.

ISBN: 978-1-9736-8633-0 (sc)
ISBN: 978-1-9736-8635-4 (hc)
ISBN: 978-1-9736-8634-7 (e)

Library of Congress Control Number: 2020903042

Print information available on the last page.

WestBow Press rev. date: 02/14/2020

I first honor and thank my Lord and Savior Jesus Christ. Because of you, I am victorious and rest in your finished works.

To my wife, Penny, whom I love with all my heart, thank you for thirty years of marriage. I appreciate all you've done and continue to do for me and the kingdom. To my two boys, James III and Joshua, my love is always and forever for you both. Thanks for helping me get the gospel out.

In honor of my mom, who is now resting in heaven, and my father, who is still serving as an example of a man of great faith and one who has a revelation of what it truly means to rest, I say thank you for shaping me into the man of faith I am today.

To my spiritual parents in the gospel for over twenty years, Dr. Creflo and Taffi Dollar, thank you for all the wisdom and impartation through our covenant connection.

To Pastor Chris Oyakhilome of Christ Embassy in South Africa, thank you for the opportunity of partnership and empowerment you have given to carry the gospel to all the world.

Last but not least, to my church family at Dunamis Christian Center, I appreciate all you do for the kingdom and your commitment to continue year after year to be faithful to the mission the Lord gave us, which is, "Releasing the power of Dunamis while preaching the gospel of grace!"

Contents

Introduction ix

Chapter 1 Grace Is Jesus 1

Chapter 2 The Finished Works of Jesus 21

Chapter 3 Exercising Your Executive Authority:
           Understanding the Principles of Natural
           and Spiritual Laws 35

Chapter 4 Throne Room Thoughts Produce Throne
           Room Realities 47

Chapter 5 Arriving at Your Final Place of Rest 63

Chapter 6 Faith Responses and Confessions That
           Bring Rest 85

Daily Faith Responses 89

Introduction

Just prior to writing this book, I was spending time in my daily prayer and meditation. The Lord began speaking to me about the importance of understanding as believers who we are in Christ, and the authority we have been given. When we understand that authority and the fact that Christ made us to be seated together with him in heavenly places, we realize we are coming from a place of victory in every situation and circumstance we face. Why? Besides the fact Christ made us to sit with him in heavenly places, every spiritual blessing we need has already been provided and is right there in the heavenly places with him! It is my desire to see the body of Christ operating from the highest place of faith and authority.

That high place of faith begins when we understand Grace, our delegated power and authority in Christ, and what it means to rest. In this book you will be given supporting scriptures to meditate on, you will learn what grace is, realize the importance of the finished works of Christ on the cross, what it means to be seated with Christ, the importance of developing throne room thoughts and speaking them, and what it means to truly rest in all this!

If you are reading this book and have never confessed Jesus as Lord and Savior but desire salvation through Grace, take a moment before going further and make this confession:

> Lord Jesus, you are the Christ, the Son of the living God. I believe you died for me and set me free. Come into my heart. Forgive me of my sins. I make you Lord and Savior of my life. Now, according to your Word, I am saved (Romans 10:9 KJV)!

Welcome to the body of believers! You are now ready to continue this Grace journey.

Chapter 1

Grace Is Jesus

John 1:14 (KJV)

John 1:17 (AMP)

Acts 13:38–39 (KJV)

Ephesians 2:8–9 (KJV)

Galatians 5:1–4 (KJV)

Meditational Scriptures

*B*efore the believer can ever enter a place of rest or total faith and trust in the finished works of Jesus on the cross, he or she must fully understand what Grace is and what Grace is not. By definition, Grace is unmerited divine assistance given to humans for their regeneration or sanctification (*Merriam-Webster* 2019). I like to define Grace as the free, undeserved, unmerited favor of God. In other words, you do not have to do anything to receive this favor except believe in God and receive.

Grace is Jesus. Grace is a person, not just a Christian notion to take lightly. Grace is not a subject or a message but a person, and his name is Jesus! The apostle Paul confirmed Grace *is* Jesus in Acts 13:38–39 (KJV), which says, "Be it known unto you therefore, men and brethren, that through this man is preached unto you the forgiveness of sins: And by his all that believe are justified from all things, from which ye could not be justified by the law of Moses." Now look at what the Amplified Bible Classic Edition (AMPC) says.

> So let it be clearly known and understood brethren that through this man forgiveness and removal of sins is now proclaimed to you; and that through Him everyone who believes [who acknowledges Jesus as his Savior and devotes himself to Him] is absolved [cleared and freed] from every charge

from which he could not be justified and freed by
the Law of Moses and given right standing with
God. (Acts 13:38–39)

Grace offers forgiveness and the removal of sins and
clearance and freedom from every charge of the law of Moses,
which was the Ten Commandments. Under the law, the wages,
or price, for sin was death. But under Grace, or our belief and
acceptance of Jesus, Paul reminds the believer in this scripture
that we are freed and cleared from any and every sin that
we have or will ever commit. Wow! Throughout the gospels,
you never read that Jesus expected those who came to him to
earn their blessings or his favor, which is Grace. Their sins (or
"missing the mark") didn't even hinder his compassion to heal
and set the captives free. Everyone who was healed, delivered,
or blessed while Jesus was ministering on the earth all had a sin
nature from fallen humankind because no one could be born
again until Jesus died on the cross and was resurrected. Being
born again does not refer to a natural birth but to a new birth
in him by confessing and accepting him as Lord and Savior.

Now back to Grace and God's blessings. The Jews believed
that one only had a relationship with God through the
Abrahamic covenant, but even if one were a Gentile with no
covenant, Jesus did not disqualify the person from experiencing

his love and compassion. He blessed and healed them all. His only requirement was to believe in him and have faith in him.

Now that you know Grace is Jesus, let's examine what Grace provides for you as a believer. Jesus is the personification of Grace, and his Grace provides the believer with unmerited, undeserved, unearned *favor*. The meditational scripture found in John 1:17 (KJV) says, "For the law was given by Moses, but grace and truth came by Jesus Christ." Now look at this same scripture in the AMPC: "For while the Law was given through Moses, grace [unearned, undeserved favor and spiritual blessing] and truth came through Jesus Christ." Notice these two versions of scripture both state that the law was *given* but Grace *came*. In other words, the law is something you do, but Grace is something you experience from a touch of humanity or compassion. The law always requires you to do something and is performance based, while Grace is never about what you do or perform. It is about what Jesus has already done. You will learn more about this in the next chapter on the finished works of Jesus. It is never about what you can do to make Grace happen. Praying, fasting, and living right are good and necessary acts that every believer should practice. However, none of them are requirements to experience God's Grace. Grace is what God has already provided for us, independent of our efforts.

Grace provides forgiveness of sins first and foremost. Human sin consciousness, or constant awareness of sin, allows Satan to put people in a mental state where they no longer seek God in prayer and fellowship, where they believe God is angry at them and will not answer their prayers. Now don't hear what I'm not saying. I am *not* saying Grace gives the believer a pass to commit sin. I am saying that God knew from the beginning of time that it would be impossible for humans to keep all the laws. There were 613 commandments. There was no possible way that humans would ever keep and obey all 613 laws. Therefore, the priests gave burnt offerings and sacrifices on behalf of the people to make atonement, or reparation, for their wrongs every year. This is what is so wonderful about Grace. When Jesus died on the cross and shed his blood, he who knew no sin became sin for humankind. He took our places. He made final atonement for all humankind so that we would never have to offer sacrifices for our sins ever again.

What Was the Purpose of the Law?

The law strengthened sin to make humanity turn to the Savior because no one could ever keep the law. First Corinthians (KJV) 15:56 says, "The sting of death is sin, and the strength of sin is the Law." In the Amplified Bible, the same verse reads,

"The sting of death is sin, and the power of sin [by which it brings death] is the law."

The law brought the people of the world to the end of themselves to say, "I cannot do this on my own. I need a Savior."

> Now we know that what things soever the law saith, it saith to them who are under the law: that every mouth may be stopped, and all the world may become guilty before God. Therefore by the deeds of the law there shall no flesh be justified in his sight: for by the law is the knowledge of sin. But now the righteousness of God without the law is manifested, being witnessed by the law and the prophets. (Romans 3:19–21 KJV)

Read the same verse in the Amplified Bible.

> Now we know that what things soever the law saith, it saith to them who are under the law: that every mouth may be stopped, and all the world may become guilty before God. Therefore by the deeds of the law there shall no flesh be justified in his sight: for by The law is the knowledge of sin. But now the righteousness of God without the law

is manifested, being witnessed by the law and the prophets. (Romans 3:19–21)

These scriptures tell us that the law came to strengthen the power of sin so that humans would be aware they needed a Savior. The law was not given to modify behavior. No, Jesus wanted humans to recognize that they would never be able to keep all the law and would need a Savior. Your effort and performance would never be perfect enough to have a true relationship with God. Look at James 2:10–11 in both the King James Version and the Amplified Bible.

> For whosoever shall keep the whole law, and yet offend in one point, he is guilty of all. For he that said, Do not commit adultery said also, Do not kill. Now if thou commit no adultery, yet if thou kill, thou art become a transgressor of the law. (KJV)

> For whoever keeps the whole Law but stumbles in one point, he has become guilty of [breaking] all of it. For He who said "Do not *commit adultery*, also said, *"Do not murder."* Now if you do not commit adultery, but you murder, you have become guilty

of transgressing the [entire] Law. (AMP; emphasis added)

These scriptures tell us if we don't keep the whole law, we are guilty of it all. So without Jesus and faith in him, no one can truly be in right standing with God. Now it may seem that because we are free from the Mosaic law Christians today are not required to live by the law. However, Jesus says there is in fact one law Christians must live by. This is the law of love. Look at John 13:34–35 (KJV): "A new commandment I give unto you, that ye love one another; as I have loved you that ye also love one another. By this shall all man know that ye are my disciples if ye have love one to another."

When Christians walk in love, they fulfill the law. Romans 13:8–10 (KJV) tells us,

> Owe no man anything, but to love one another: for he that liveth another hath fulfilled the law. For this, Thou shalt not commit adultery, Thou shalt not kill, Thou shalt not steal, Thou shalt not bear false witness, Thou shalt not covet; and if there any other commandment, it is briefly comprehended in this saying, namely Thou shalt

9

love thy neighbor as thyself. Love worketh no ill to
his neighbor: thee love is the fulfilling of the law.

What else does Grace provide? Ephesians 2:8–9 (KJV) says
that when a believer confesses and receives salvation, it is, "For
by grace are ye saved through faith; and that not of yourselves:
it is the gift of God: Not of works, lest any man should boast."

Now look at that same scripture in the Amplified version:
"For it is by free grace (God's unmerited favor) that you are
saved ([a]delivered from judgment *and* made partakers of
Christ's salvation) through [your] faith. And this [salvation] is
not of yourselves [of your own doing, it came not through your
own striving], but it is the gift of God; Not because of works
[not the fulfillment of the Law's demands], lest any man should
boast. [It is not the result of what anyone can possibly do, so no
one can pride himself in it or take glory to himself.]"

The Greek word for saved is *Sozo*. Sozo is forgiveness, healing,
deliverance, soundness, wholeness, and all the finished works of
Jesus. So by Grace, you are saved through faith, not by works.
Salvation is a gift from God. Grace provides salvation.

Now let's look at Matthew 8:5–13 (KJV). In this scripture,
we find a Gentile man who came to Jesus. By law, he had no
right to receive healing because of the old covenant dispensation
of the law and because he was not a Jew. In the Old Testament,

only the Jews were qualified to receive blessings. This man was the well-known centurion who made a plea to Jesus to heal his servant, who was lying at home paralyzed, "suffering terribly." Jesus said that this centurion had "great faith." Why? Because he had a revelation that Grace was standing before him in that moment in the form of Jesus, and was not only able to heal his servant but willing to heal his servant by just speaking a word. Grace provides healing. In Matthew 8:16–17 (KJV), Jesus healed all who came to him and never questioned their imperfections or sins. These healings were unmerited. In Luke 6:17–19 (KJV), we find a whole multitude receiving at one time as they believed and even touched his garment. How much sin do you think was in the midst of Jesus at that moment? Jesus never addressed the sin; he simply allowed his power to heal them all.

God knows we sometimes fall short of reaching the mark. His love is so unconditional that Jesus found himself blessing humanity with unmerited favor! Don't get me wrong. Even though Jesus was full of compassion and mercy and offered Grace, he reminded those in the midst of sin to "go and sin no more." Jesus was teaching that sin will make every effort to keep you bound every day, leaving an inroad or opening for Satan to come into your life. Eventually, this draws you away from the very one who offers Grace—Jesus. The woman caught amid adultery finds forgiveness through Grace, but not without Jesus reminding her to go and sin no more.

Look at John 8:3–11 (KJV).

> And the scribes and Pharisees brought unto him a woman taken in adultery; and when they had set her in the midst They say unto him, Master, this woman was taken in adultery, in the very act. Now Moses in the law commanded us, that such should be stoned: but what sayest thou? This they said, tempting him, that they might have to accuse him. But Jesus stooped down, and with his finger wrote on the ground, as though he heard them not. So when they continued asking him, he lifted up himself, and said unto them, He that is without sin among you, let him first cast a stone at her. And again he stooped down, and wrote on the ground. And they which heard it, being convicted by their own conscience, went out one by one, beginning at the eldest, even unto the last: and Jesus was left alone, and the woman standing in the midst. When Jesus had lifted up himself, and saw none but the woman, he said unto her, Woman, where are those thine accusers? hath no

man condemned thee? She said, No man, Lord.

And Jesus said unto her, Neither do I condemn

thee: go, and sin no more.

In other words, Grace forgives you, woman, but if you continue in the sin, you will find yourself bound again and the door will be open for Satan to be at work in your life. Religion condemns, but Grace forgives. So receive this Grace, and then do not practice sin anymore. Jesus reminds us today that while his blood has wiped out every sin we ever could or would commit, do not practice sin because of Grace. We must understand that Grace provides a means to be free from the practice of sin. While the believer should always strive to live holy, Romans 6:1–3 (KJV) explains how the believer can abstain from sin: "What shall we say then? Shall we continue in sin, that grace may abound? God forbid. How shall we, that are dead to sin, live any longer therein? Know ye not, that so many of us as were baptized into Jesus Christ were baptized into his death?"

Human sin nature changes when a person becomes a believer. The individual is a new creature. Therefore, as a new creature, the believer's nature, or innate quality or character, is to only please God. So now, even if you miss the mark, there is no peace for a believer until the person repents and turns away from that sin in one's heart. The believer does not become condemned before God, but the desire is there to stay in continuous fellowship with the Savior. Look at Romans 6:14 (KJV): "For sin shall not have dominion over you: for ye are not under the law, but under grace." This scripture reminds believers that under Grace, we are not controlled or dominated by sin anymore because Jesus gave us the authority to resist the devil. When we resist, we ignore the attraction or temptation of sin, which causes the devil to flee. This resistance is only possible because we have new natures and believe in Jesus. Religion says I can keep one of the commandments of the law, which somehow makes me okay in the eyes of God. No, that is what we call Christian-based performance, or trying to use the works performed by flesh (humans) and self-effort, to reach the goal of righteousness. I was listening to a message recently by my spiritual father, Dr. Creflo Dollar. Dr. Dollar made a profound statement about the law versus being led by the Spirit. He said, "The Holy Spirit inside of the believer will now begin to govern morality," meaning the Holy Spirit will now lead the believer to do what is right morally. When someone or something is governed, it is controlled or influenced. So the Holy Spirit inside every believer always leads us to do what is morally right, but because we are moral free agents, we still sometimes get in our flesh and do wrong things.

The apostle Paul understood this when he mentioned in Romans 7:15 (AMP), "For I do not understand my own actions [I am baffled and bewildered by them]. I do not practice *what I want to do, but I am doing the very thing I hate [and yielding to my human nature, my worldliness-my sinful capacity"* (emphasis added). Paul understood that he had a choice to yield to the spirit or the flesh.

The believer must know and understand what Grace is and what it is not. Grace is the dispensation that we are under now. Grace is not the law, which was for the Jews. Grace is for everyone, including the Gentiles. The Word of God says where sin abounds, Grace does much more abound. So when the scripture speaks of "falling from grace," it is not saying you messed up and fell into sin, so now Grace is not extended to you. Paul reminded the Galatians to stand in the liberty whereby Christ made them free. He was speaking against the law of circumcision that said unless you were circumcised, you were not special or set apart. Paul was reminding the people that they were now under the dispensation of Grace, and the law no longer applied or was necessary to receive God's Grace. If you do not have this revelation, that is when you may fall from Grace. So today, as believers, we must be careful not to "fall into" this same mind-set of the law and "fall from" the Grace that God so freely gives. Again, the law was not made for a righteous people but for the unrighteous to show their need of a Savior. This is why the gospels are nearly too good to be true news of Grace and must be preached and understood by all who accept Jesus as their Savior. Remember this, my friend, under the law before Jesus, God was a judge; but under Grace, he is a loving Father. God is not this mean person waiting to judge us for our sins. Judgment is a done deal for the believer, and you must know this before praying. Ephesians 2:8 (AMP) says,

> For it is by grace [God's remarkable compassion and favor drawing you to Christ] that you have been saved [actually delivered from judgment and given eternal life] through faith. And this [salvation] is not of yourselves [not through your own effort], but it is the [undeserved, gracious] gift of God; not as a result of [your] works [nor your attempts to keep the Law], so that no one will [be able to] boast *or* take credit in any way [for his salvation]. (emphasis added)

Another scripture to read is John 3:18 (AMP).

> Whoever believes *and* has decided to trust in Him [as personal Savior and Lord] is not judged [for

this one, there is no judgment, no rejection, no condemnation]; but the one who does not believe [and has decided to reject Him as personal Savior and Lord] is judged already [that one has been convicted and sentenced], because [a]he has not believed *and* trusted in the name of the [One and] only begotten Son of God [the One who is truly unique, the only One of His kind, the One who alone can save him]. (emphasis added)

A familiar passage of scripture that is often misinterpreted is John 12:29. This scripture references Jesus taking on the judgment of the entire world. John 12:29–41(AMP) says,

The crowd *of people* who stood nearby and heard the voice said that it had thundered; others said, "An angel has spoken to Him!" Jesus answered, "This voice has come for your sake, not for mine. Now judgment is upon this world [the sentence is being passed]. Now the ruler of this world (Satan) will be cast out. And I, if *and* when I am lifted up from the earth [on the cross], will draw all *people* to Myself [Gentiles, as well as Jews]." He said this to indicate the kind of death by which he was to die. At this the crowd answered Him, "[a]We have heard from the Law that the Christ is to remain forever; how then can You say, 'The Son of Man must be lifted up'? Who is this Son of Man?" So Jesus said to them, "The Light is among you [only] a little while longer. Walk while you have the Light [keep on living by it], so that darkness will not overtake you. He who walks in the darkness does not know where he is going [he is drifting aimlessly]. While you have the Light, believe *and* trust in the Light [have faith in it, hold on to it, rely on it], so that you may become sons of Light [being filled with Light as followers of God]." (emphasis added)

Jesus was saying he would draw everyone's judgments unto him. There is nothing on earth you can do that he has not already died for. As a believer, one must totally depend on Jesus. Grace only responds with dependence on Jesus.

Now look at Galatians 2:19–21 in the Message Bible.

What actually took place is this: I tried keeping rules and working my head off to please God, and it didn't work. So I quit being a "law man" so that I could be *God's* man. Christ's life showed me how, and enabled me to do it. I identified myself completely with him. Indeed, I have been crucified with Christ. My ego is no longer central. It is no longer important that I appear righteous before you or have your good opinion, and I am no longer driven to impress God. Christ lives in me. The life you see me living is not "mine," but it is lived by faith in the Son of God, who loved me and gave himself for me. I am not going to go back on that. Is it not clear to you that to go back to that old rule-keeping, peer-pleasing religion would be an abandonment of everything personal and free in my relationship with God? I refuse to do that, to *repudiate God's grace.* If a living relationship with God could come by rule-keeping, then Christ died unnecessarily. (emphasis added)

What if the believer took the same stance as Paul? God inspired Paul to write over half of the New Testament. Paul was adamant about his personal relationship with God. Paul had a revelation that the relationship he shared with God was one of Grace, not the law. Paul ends the scripture by saying he refused to abandon everything personal and free in his relationship with God. He refused to repudiate or go back on what Grace provided by trying to keep rules, do works, and appear righteous before humans. Paul said he had already tried all that, and since it didn't work, he quit being a "law man." He made the decision to have a personal relationship with God and received this Grace, this free, undeserved, unmerited favor and goodness of God. Make the decision today to be a God man or woman and not a law man or woman.

Chapter 2

The Finished Works of Jesus

John 19:30 (KJV)

Romans 1:16–17

Ephesians 1:3 (AMP)

Psalm 103:1–3 (KJV)

2 Peter 1:3–4 (KJV)

Hebrews 9:11–15 (KJV)

Hebrews 9:24–26 (AMP)

Hebrews 10:10–19 (KJV)

Colossians 2:9–15 (KJV)

Acts 14:3–10 (KJV)

Meditational Scriptures

*N*ow that you understand Grace and the fact that Grace is Jesus, let's talk about the finished works of Jesus when he died on the cross for humankind. The meditational scriptures for this chapter will give you more insight as to what you received as a believer through the finished works, from power and authority delegated by Jesus to the fullness of the Deity in bodily form. The finished works of Jesus were brought through the sacrifice of his body as an offering once and for all for the sins of humankind. Now when God looks at us, he sees the blood of his Son, Jesus, who made a final atonement for humankind. The enemy constantly reminds us of our shortcomings, pasts, and sins, but the blood of Jesus on the cross reminds humankind that we have right standing with God in spite of any shortcomings, in spite of sins past and present. God knew humankind would never be able to keep all the law and be perfect, but his Son would be the sacrifice to provide redemption and total forgiveness of human sins, past, present, and future. That is Grace, that is love, that is Jesus!

The finished works of Jesus on the cross are what he has already done. There is nothing you can do to add to it or improve it. It is already done. Everything we could ever need as believers was provided when Jesus died on that cross over two thousand years ago, including forgiveness of our sins. The finished work of Jesus was God's ultimate provision for humankind. For death, he gave us life eternal, for sickness and health, for poverty and wealth, for defeat and victory! This is total provision for the believer, which comes to us continually by Grace! The only requirement is to believe in Jesus, and we will have access to his provision.

When Jesus shed his precious blood on that cross, he said, "It is finished!" What he was saying to the believer was that every spiritual blessing is provided to you when you believe in him and accept him as Lord and Savior of your life. Romans 10:9 (KJV), which is a familiar passage of scripture referenced in the beginning of this book, leads the unsaved to salvation. It says, "That if thou shalt confess with thy mouth the Lord Jesus, and shalt believe in thine heart that God hath raised him from the dead, thou shalt be saved. For with the heart man believeth unto righteousness; and with the mouth confession is made unto salvation." So when we confess Jesus as Lord, we believe in righteousness. Christ makes us righteous immediately, not through our works or performances, but because we believe in him. This places every believer in the right position to receive all Jesus's finished works. The Bible says we receive everything that pertains to life and godliness. Think about that; everything in this life you could ever want has already been provided.

Because of this, there is no struggle to serve God and develop an intimate, personal relationship with him.

When Jesus declared, "It is finished," on the cross, I believe that was one of his most important declarations to humankind. Why? Because it assured humankind total victory in spite of the fall of Adam. Under old covenant law, the Jews had to work and perform to have a relationship with the Father. If they qualified and kept God's commandments, they would receive the blessings of God. But if they were not perfect, they would have to kill an animal, and the animal's blood was symbolic of covering their sins. The people did this year after year.

Look at Deuteronomy 28:1–2 (KJV): "And it shall come to pass, if thou shalt hearken diligently unto the voice of the Lord thy God, to observe and to do all his commandments which I command thee this day, that the Lord thy God will set thee on high above all nations of the earth: And all these blessings shall come on thee, and overtake thee, if thou shalt hearken unto the voice of the Lord thy God." Deuteronomy 28:15 (KJV) says, "But it shall come to pass, if thou wilt not hearken unto the voice of the Lord thy God, to observe to do all his commandments and his statutes which I command thee this day; that all these curses shall come upon thee, and overtake thee."

So in these scriptures, we see that the people were told they would be blessed (empowered to prosper) if they observed all the commandments and cursed (empowered to fail) if they did not. Through priests, they offered sacrifices for their sins year after year because no one was able to keep all the commandments. Glory to God! Jesus set us free through his blood and finished works on the cross.

Look at Galatians 3:10–13 (KJV).

> For as many as are of the works of the law are under the curse: for it is written, Cursed is every one that continueth not in all things which are written in the book of the law to do them. But that no man is justified by the law in the sight of God, it is evident: for, The just shall live by faith. And the law is not of faith: but, The man that doeth them shall live in them. Christ hath redeemed us from the curse of the law, being made a curse for us: for it is written, Cursed is every one that hangeth on a tree.

This scripture confirms the importance of our Savior Jesus completing the finished works. The Ten Commandments and the 613 laws required perfection that always left humankind in condemnation and guilt. But Jesus not only redeemed us from the curse of the law, he also made available to the believer all blessings under the new covenant dispensation of Grace. These blessings and freedom from condemnation and guilt are not based on works or self-efforts. They are based on total dependence on Jesus and his finished works on the cross. This belief and dependence must be established or planted inside you as a believer.

Let's look at some more examples of the finished works. Hebrews 9:11–15 (KJV) says,

> But Christ being come a high priest of good things to come, by a greater and more perfect tabernacle, not made with hands, that is to say, not of this building; Neither by the blood of goats and calves, but by his own blood he entered in once into the holy place, having obtained eternal redemption for us. For if the blood of bulls and of goats, and the ashes of an heifer sprinkling the unclean, sanctifieth to the purifying of the flesh: How much more shall the blood of Christ, who through the eternal Spirit offered himself without spot to God, purge your conscience from dead works to serve the living God? And for this cause he is the mediator of the new testament,

that by means of death, for the redemption of the transgressions that were under the first testament, they which are called might receive the promise of eternal inheritance.

This scripture tells us that Jesus once went in to the holy place (just like the priests did in the Old Testament, when they went into the Holy Temple to offer sacrifices for humankind). The Amplified version says he went in "once for all," having found and secured a complete redemption or a finished redemption, an everlasting release for us, purging our consciences from dead works or works of the flesh that you would called performance based Christianity.

Look specifically at verse 15 of Hebrews chapter 9 in the Amplified version: "For this reason He is the Mediator *and* Negotiator of a new covenant [that is, an entirely new agreement uniting God and man], so that those who have been called [by God] may receive [the fulfillment of] the promised eternal inheritance, since a death has taken place [as the payment] which redeems them from the sins *committed* under the *obsolete* first covenant" (emphasis added).

What is a mediator? It is one who stands in the gap to bring reconciliation and better promises through an inheritance.

Jesus's inheritance is an eternal one. In other words, it is finished forever!

I want you to look at this same scripture in the Mirror Bible, which explains further the fact that Jesus is now our high priest who offered a sacrifice for all our sins, past, present, and future. This sacrifice was not based on the blood of animals, like the priests offered in the Old Testament, but by the blood of Jesus. One act, once and for all, in the most sacred place of Grace provides an eternal, inherited promise of forgiveness!

> But now Christ has made his public appearance as High Priest of a perfect tabernacle. The good things that were predicted have arrived. This new tabernacle does not derive from its shadow type, the previous man-made one. It is the reality. (The restoration of God's original dwelling place in human life is again revealed!) As High Priest, his permission to enter the Holy Place was not secured by the blood of beasts. By his own blood he obtained access on behalf of the human race. Only one act was needed for him to enter the most sacred place of grace and there to institute a ransom of perpetual consequence. (The perfection of the redemption he secured needs no

further sacrifice. There are no outstanding debts; there is nothing we need do to add weight to what he has accomplished once and for all. The only possible priesthood activity we can now engage in is to continually bring a sacrifice of the fruit of our lips, giving thanks to his Name; no blood, just fruit, even our acts of self-sacrifice, giving of time and money, etc. are all just the fruit of our constant gratitude!) The blood of beasts and the ashes of the burnt sacrifice of a heifer could only achieve a very temporal and surface cleansing by being sprinkled on the guilty. (Hebrews 9:11–15 Mirror Bible)

Now look at Hebrews 10:12 (KJV):

By the which will *we are sanctified through the offering of the body of Jesus Christ once for all.* And every priest standeth daily ministering and offering oftentimes the same sacrifices, which can never take away sins: But this man, after *he had offered one sacrifice for sins for ever,* sat down on the right hand of God; From henceforth expecting till his enemies be made his footstool. *For by one offering he hath perfected for ever them that are sanctified.* (emphasis added)

The scripture says after Jesus offered one sacrifice for sins forever, he, "sat down on the right hand of God!" The finished works were established when he sat down. Jesus sat down because he finished everything on the cross. What does that mean for the believer? Well, Ephesians 2:6 (KJV) says, "And hath raised us up together, and made us sit together in heavenly places in Christ Jesus." As believers we have been made to sit in heavenly places in him. Not beside him, *in* him. This means we have the same power and authority that he has. The Mirror Bible tells us we share executive authority. When we understand as believers what the finished works of Jesus on the cross provided, we are able to operate as kingdom citizens, exercising our executive authority by enforcing the laws of heaven here on earth. In the natural, a judge in court exercises his or her executive authority to enforce the laws of the land. No one questions the judge's delegated authority; they just obey. As believers, we must understand that, like a judge in a court of law, we have delegated executive authority just like Jesus because he made us to sit in him in heavenly places. When we realize this, we can begin to speak to our situations and circumstances and command them to change. "As it is in heaven," so can it be here on earth. When we understand what the finished works of Jesus have provided, our mind-sets change. When Jesus sat down, he confirmed this work finished and provided the believer with a rest in forgiveness, healing, deliverance, safety, soundness, protection, and preservation.

The apostle Paul was sold on the concept of Grace and the finished works of Jesus. Look at what he says about this in Galatians 2:19–21 in the Message Bible:

> What actually took place is this: I tried keeping rules and working my head off to please God, and it didn't work. So I quit being a "law man" so that I could be *God's* man. Christ's life showed me how, and enabled me to do it. I identified myself completely with him. Indeed, I have been crucified with Christ. My ego is no longer central. It is no longer important that I appear righteous before you or have your good opinion, and I am no longer driven to impress God. Christ lives in me. The life you see me living is not "mine," but it is lived by faith in the Son of God, who loved me and gave himself for me. I am not going to go back on that.

Is it not clear to you that to go back to that old rule-keeping, peer-pleasing religion would be an abandonment of everything personal and free in my relationship with God? I refuse to do that, to repudiate God's grace. If a living relationship with God could come by rule-keeping, then Christ died unnecessarily. (emphasis added)

Wow! Paul was sold on Grace and the finished works of Jesus. Paul had a revelation of what was provided to the believer because of the finished works of Jesus. Paul understood when he said he kept trying to keep rules and work hard to please God. All he really needed to do was believe in Jesus and his finished works, quit trying to do the law, and accept this Grace Jesus so freely gives. That is why Paul became one of the most powerful apostles to deliver this gospel, or nearly too good to be true good news about the Grace of our Lord Jesus Christ.

Chapter 3

Exercising Your Executive Authority: Understanding the Principles of Natural and Spiritual Laws

Mark 16:15–17

John 14:13

Ephesians 2:6

Ephesians 1:20–23

Proverbs 18:21

Meditational Scriptures

*S*o we understand what Grace has provided through the finished works of Jesus on the cross and the fact that we are no longer regulated by the law. We are now in the dispensation of Grace. Now let's talk about exercising this authority Jesus gave us by Grace and faith in him. In order to fully exercise our authority as believers, we must first understand the delegation of this authority. Let's look at where this delegated authority began. Mark 16:15–17 (KJV) says, "And he said unto them, Go ye into all the world, and preach the gospel to every creature. He that believeth and is baptized shall be saved; but he that believeth not shall be damned. And these signs shall follow them that believe; In my name shall they cast out devils; they shall speak with new tongues." This passage of scripture is referred to as the Great Commission to believers. Note the last verse: "in my name." This is where Jesus gave the believer the delegated authority to use/exercise his name and operate *like him* here on earth.

Now look at another example, this one found in John 14:13 (AMP): "And I will do whatever you ask in My name [[a]*as My representative*], this I will do, so that the Father may be glorified *and* celebrated in the Son" (emphasis added). Again, Jesus is saying, "Use my name as my representative." Now that we understand that we have been given delegated authority by

Jesus to operate here on earth just like he does, let's talk about exercising this executive authority from our seated place in him. This will also help us understand how this executive authority governs natural and spiritual laws.

We see in Ephesians 2:6 (AMP) that the believer has been raised up with Christ and is seated with him in heavenly places: "And He raised us up together with Him [when we believed], and seated us with Him in the heavenly *places*, [because we are] in Christ Jesus." Why is it so important to understand this seat we have in Christ Jesus? Look at Ephesians 1:20–23 (AMP). It says,

> which He [a]produced in Christ when He raised Him from the dead and seated Him at His own right hand in the heavenly *places*, far above all rule and authority and power and dominion [whether angelic or human], and [far above] every name that is named [above every title that can be conferred], not only in this age *and* world but also in the one to come. And He [b]put all things [in every realm] in subjection under Christ's feet, and [c]appointed Him as [supreme and authoritative] head over all things in the church, which is His

body, the fullness of Him who fills *and* completes

all things in all [believers]. (emphasis added)

Are you beginning to understand not only this delegated authority you have been given as a believer but the position of authority you are in because of being "seated in Him [Christ Jesus]"? Ephesians 1:20–23 (KJV) tells us that not only did God raise Christ from the dead, he seated him at his own right hand in heavenly places. We share in this seated place of authority because, as mentioned above, we are raised up and seated with him! Look closely at verse 21. This verse reminds us that not only are we seated with/in him, but because he is far above every name that is named, every title, all rule, authority, power, and dominion—whether angelic or human—so are we as believers! God put everything under Christ's feet and appointed him as the supreme authority over all. Say aloud, "As Christ is, so am I!"

Let's now discuss what exactly this position of joint seating means. The moment we received Jesus as Lord and Savior, we became alive, and eternal life began to move inside us. We then became "seated together with Christ Jesus in heavenly places" (Ephesians 2:6 KJV). This joint seating with him means that in the spiritual realm, we have the same executive authority that God gave Jesus when he raised him from the dead and set him at his own right hand. This was not literally his right hand in location but symbolically as a place of power. As believers, this executive authority is delegated power, the right to command or exercise dominion in heaven and earth, and the power to execute and enforce the laws of God's Word. In other words, anything that is not the will of God, which is his Word, the believer can change with prayers, decrees, and commands. The believer's words through prayers, decrees, and commands are powerful. So much so that Proverbs 18:21 speaks of life and death being in the power of the tongue. Look at this scripture in the Message Bible: "Words kill, words give life; they're either poison or fruit—you choose." Not only does the Bible tell us about the power of our words, God ends by saying, "You choose." So the believer has a choice in the matter by the words he or she speaks. Taking all this into account, when the believer understands his or her delegated authority and position of power in Christ, exercising this executive authority while understanding the principles of natural and spiritual laws becomes easy.

Let's talk a little about spiritual versus natural laws. Spiritual laws are different than the Mosaic laws we discussed in chapters 1 and 2. First, let's define the word *law.* *Law* is defined as "a rule or order that it is advisable or obligatory to observe" (*Merriam-Webster* 2019).

A judge in the world system has executive authority to enforce the law or rules of the land in a court system. The judge makes the final decree/decision when he or she hands down the sentence following a verdict. As believers in the kingdom of God, we have this same executive authority given to us by Jesus to enforce the laws of heaven, which are spiritual laws, here on earth to change natural laws. If in the natural we are experiencing sickness in our bodies, we take the Word of God and speak healing over our bodies. Like a judge in a courtroom, we remind the devil, "By His stripes I am healed!" This is our final decree. It is not based on what we see or what we feel in our bodies at the time. It is not based on the doctor's report of gloom and doom. We make a final decree because God said it, we believe, and his Word is forever settled in heaven! I believe when we begin to operate in this kind of faith in God's Word, we will see the manifestation of what we pray and speak according to the spiritual laws of God's Word.

Another example I want to share involves why God blesses who he does. Believers often wonder how "worldly" people can be blessed by God. I have read many testimonies of Hollywood stars who shared that before they ever became famous, they wrote down what it was that they wanted to achieve. They looked at it every day and believed it would happen. This is a facet of something the world refers to this as the law of attraction. As believers, we can reference several scriptures that deal with that question. Habakkuk 2:2 (NKJV) says, "Then the Lord answered me and said: Write the vision And make it plain on tablets, that he may run who reads it. For the vision is yet for an appointed time; But at the end it will speak, and it will not lie. Though it tarries, wait for it; Because it will surely come, it will not tarry." This is "writing the vision" of what we are expecting. Not only that, Mark 9:23 (AMP) reminds us that "all things are possible," and the only requirement is our belief. "Jesus said to him, "If[a] you can believe, all things are possible to him who believes." Note the scripture does not say all things are possible to them who believe and are saved.

You should now have an understanding of your executive authority as a believer and the difference between a natural law and a spiritual law. I want to share a personal testimony about executive authority. While there are so many testimonies I could share about operating in this executive authority, here is one that I will never forget. This was a season of my life when I knew that if God did not do anything for me that I asked in prayer, independent of my effort, it would not have been done. I am grateful and thankful that God has allowed me to celebrate twenty years of ministry. We began in a local hotel with only eight people. God taught me early on how to believe totally in Jesus and release executive authority. I took a picture of a $2.1 million building that God showed me would be my church. Even though I knew it would be a process to obtain it, I took it on as a faith project. At the end of every Sunday service, I had the congregation and visitors point to a picture we had of the building, believing and trusting in God's Grace that he had already made a way out of no way. We were standing in faith, but everything seemed to go wrong and go against us purchasing the property. But I stayed in faith. Every day I drove to the parking lot and sat in front of the building, by faith, I imagined I was sitting in my office . I would begin speaking to the building in faith, and calling it from the spiritual realm, to natural ownership in my life by my speaking. Now mind you we did not have the money, nor did any bank want to approve us for a loan because they thought we were too young of a congregation to purchase a million-dollar church. I kept doing this daily for two years, and one day after feeling different emotions about not knowing how this seemingly impossible miracle was going to take place, I sat in my car, meditating on Romans 10:11 (NKJV): "For the Scripture says, 'Whoever believes on Him will not be put to shame.'" While reading and meditating on this scripture, my wife called and said someone had called the house out of the blue. And when she said the caller had the wrong number, the person began to give a prophecy to her and asked, "Is your husband a pastor?" She replied yes, and the person told her to tell me that God said, "I'll never put him to shame!" It was the exact phrase I'd been reading right before she called. I never forgot that moment. It fueled and encouraged me during the rest of the process, and it later became my response to everything. You see, faith is a positive response to what Grace has already provided. I began to respond differently, saying, "In the name of Jesus, he will never put me to shame or disappoint me!" I was then led to ask the owners of the building if we, as a church, could rent the building until we were able to purchase it. Their initial response was no. They only wanted to sell it, but if we could pay $5,000 a week, or $20,000 monthly, they would allow it. I honestly believe that because it seemed impossible, the owners thought I would get discouraged and go away. Instead, I rose up and declared, "God will never put me to shame or disappoint me!" Well, guess what? They allowed us in the building with a stipulation that we could not be late on a payment. They told me I could not have a key; someone would let me in every Wednesday and Sunday. And I could not put up a sign until I actually purchased the building. God supernaturally met every need for two and a half years of renting. Eventually, the owners and I met again, and they said they had changed their minds, and no longer wanted to hold us up from ministry. Their exact words to me were, "Surely the Lord is with you." They gave me the keys and told me I could put our sign up. They took all our rent payments and applied them to the down payment to purchase the building. Glory to God! While we still face troubles and difficulties in ministry, we still worship and praise the Lord Jesus Christ for his Grace and faithfulness. I have been convinced of the fact that God will never put me to shame or disappoint me. My friend, this testimony was not to boast or say by any means that any of this was because of my self-effort. This was to demonstrate how powerfully our Lord works on our behalf when we totally believe in him. I exercised my executive authority by speaking the Word only, staying in faith, and trusting God. Then I rested in what I believed. In the natural it looked like I would never get what I was hoping for, but I continued to exercise a spiritual law of speaking faith to the situation, and the spiritual laws of confession brought possession of what I believed in.

In the next chapter, we take this understanding of authority and apply principles of both natural and spiritual laws to create "throne room" thoughts that promote a place of rest in the finished works of Christ and the reality or manifestation of what we believe.

Chapter 4

Throne Room Thoughts Produce Throne Room Realities

2 Corinthians 10:5 (KJV)

Colossians 3:1–3

Mark 4:35–41

Mark 11:23

John 14:12–14

Meditational Scriptures

Our daily thoughts or what we choose to meditate on can be the difference between producing strongholds in our lives and creating throne room realities. A stronghold is formed when we allow negative thoughts to enter our minds, and instead of casting them down as the Word of God instructs us to do in 2 Corinthians 10:5, we allow these negative thoughts to make their permanent resting places in our minds and, eventually, in our hearts. These negative thoughts, or strongholds, make it virtually impossible to have faith in the Word of God. They cause doubt, unbelief, and move us in a direction of fear instead of faith.

For this reason, believers must have an understanding of what it means to be raised up and seated together with Christ. Hopefully, you gained an understanding of this in the previous chapters. Understanding this reality of being seated in Christ in heavenly places is the difference between producing thoughts that lead to doubt and thoughts that produce realities and, ultimately, rest! You are probably wondering, *What is a throne room thought?* I first ran across this concept when I looked up Colossians 3:1–3 in the Mirror Bible. It reads, "See yourselves co-seated with Christ, now ponder with persuasion the consequences for your inclusion in Him Relocate yourselves mentally, enlarge your thoughts with Throne Room Realities where you are co-seated with Christ in the Executive Authority of God's right hand. Becoming affectionately acquainted with Throne room thoughts will keep you from being distracted again by the earthy ruled soul-realm."

Wow! Go back and read that again. As a matter of fact, begin to meditate on this scripture daily. Say it aloud; faith comes by hearing. Let's start with the beginning of this verse. It says to see yourselves co-seated with Christ. Before you can even begin to create throne room thoughts, you must see yourself in the spirit seated in Christ. Now look at the next sentence: "ponder with persuasion the consequences for your inclusion in Him." To ponder is to think about something carefully, especially before reaching a conclusion.

Now that you see yourself seated in him, think about what that means before you reach a conclusion of doubt that what he said in his Word, which you have been meditating on, will actually come to pass in your life. Okay, so now we see ourselves spiritually seated in him. We are thinking carefully about what this means, so we do not allow doubt to creep in. Then we can think about this reality of being seated in him in faith instead of doubt. The effect, or consequences, of our inclusion in Christ, seated in him in heavenly places, will now affect or become the consequences of what we believe. Our faith in being seated in him can cause us to relocate ourselves mentally or relocate our thoughts, which will become enlarged with throne room realities.

Our thoughts produce realities in the natural, so why not allow them to produce throne room realities? A reality is something that is experienced or seen. When we begin to meditate on God's Word daily, we will begin to produce throne room realities in our lives. Not only that, we can avoid being distracted from all God has for us in this life by creating throne room realities inside us. How is this accomplished? Throne room realities are birthed through meditation. What is meditation? Meditation is when you find the scripture that covers what you are seeking God for; I like to refer to it as finding the scripture that "covers your case." Remember, we are operating in spiritual laws. Like any good attorney, we search for and find the laws or the Word of God that covers our cases. This word makes our cases solid ones that win in the court of law! Now that we have found the scriptures that cover our cases, we begin to think on and say them over and over again until faith comes. How do we know when faith comes? We begin to see what we have been meditating on. We can see it inside us as pictures in our spirits before they even manifest in the natural.

I want to share some throne room meditations. God gave me

four realities that will place us in positions of rest and victory. These four realities are straight from the scripture in the Mirror Bible, which we broke down earlier in this chapter.

1. See yourself coseated with Christ.
2. Enlarge your thoughts with throne room realities (God's Word/promises).
3. See yourself with executive authority through the use of his name.
4. Become affectionately acquainted and rest in him. *Affectionately* means a way that displays fondness or tenderness. It is about relationship. When we develop a personal relationship by spending time with God and his Word, we become so acquainted with him and his love for us that we can now rest in his promises.

Now, let's discuss a little the fact that creating throne room realities from meditating on the Word of God can actually help the believer overcome every storm of life.

Look at Mark 4:35–41 (KJV). It says,

> And the same day, when the even was come, he saith unto them, Let us pass over unto the other side. And when they had sent away the multitude,

they took him even as he was in the ship. And there were also with him other little ships. And there arose a great storm of wind, and the waves beat into the ship, so that it was now full. And he was in the hinder part of the ship, asleep on a pillow: and they awake him, and say unto him, Master, carest thou not that we perish? And he arose, and rebuked the wind, and said unto the sea, Peace, be still. And the wind ceased, and there was a great calm. And he said unto them, Why are ye so fearful? how is it that ye have no faith? And they feared exceedingly, and said one to another, What manner of man is this, that even the wind and the sea obey him?

This is an awesome example in the Bible of how Jesus took authority over the storm that was trying to destroy them. First, he told the disciples to get in the boat and said they were going to the other side. He gave the command, expecting them to believe in him enough to trust his promise that they were going to the other side, in spite of any storm sent by the enemy that tried to destroy them. When the enemy sends storms, which are distractions to get us not to trust the Word of God, many of us take our eyes off Jesus (the Word) and put them on the trouble we see and feel with our natural senses. This is what the disciples did.

In another translation of this scripture, it says a furious windstorm of hurricane proportions came. All hope seemed to be gone, and out of fear, the disciples woke up Jesus. They asked him if he even cared if they perished. First of all, I believe the statement about them perishing surprised Jesus. He never said anything at the beginning about perishing. Jesus said, "We are going to the other side." So Jesus rose up, rebuked the storm, and then asked the disciples, "Why are you so fearful? How is it that you have no faith?" The Amplified version of this scripture says, "Why are you so timid and fearful, and how is it that you have no faith (no firmly relying trust)." In other words, where are your throne room reality thoughts?

In this story, Jesus brings out three important keys to overcoming any storm in life.

1. Get yourself in a position of rest. Do this by developing confidence in the finished works of Jesus. See, I believe pre-cross, Jesus wanted the disciples to trust and rest in what he said: "We are going to the other side." But post-cross, in this dispensation, he wants us to trust and rest in not only what he says but what he has already done. In John 19:30 (KJV), while Jesus was on the cross, he said,

"It is finished!" Everything we could ever desire, want, or need was finished on the cross. Victory for the believer and defeat of the enemy were finished on the cross. So now the enemy can only make suggestions to try to get us out of faith in God's Word and the finished works of Jesus on the cross. What did Jesus do? He died, arose on the third day, and is now seated in heavenly places, where he has, "blessed us with all spiritual blessings in Christ" (Ephesians 1:3 KJV). So whatever we need is already done. Glory!

2. Exercise executive authority in his name. Notice when the disciples woke Jesus up, he didn't say, "Leave me alone. I am going back to sleep," or "It will be okay. I've already spoken the word." Jesus knew if he didn't do something about the situation, the storm would not stop. You see, sometimes we need to stop talking to God about the problem and speak to the problem. Don't talk to God about how big your storm is. Talk to your storm and tell it how big your God is (Mark 11:23)! This is an example of a throne room reality that every believer should have in the kingdom of God. Yes, we have authority over every storm in the name of Jesus. John 14:12–14 (KJV) says, "Verily, verily, I say unto you, He that believeth on me, the works that I do shall he do also; and greater works

than these shall he do; because I go unto my Father. And whatsoever ye shall ask in my name, that will I do, that the Father may be glorified in the Son. If ye shall ask any thing in my name, I will do it." Now, look at this same scripture in the Message Bible:

> Believe me: I am in my Father and my Father is in me. If you can't believe that, believe what you see—these works. The person who trusts me will not only do what I'm doing but even greater things, because I, on my way to the Father, am giving you the same work to do that I've been doing. You can count on it. From now on, whatever you request along the lines of who I am and what I am doing, I'll do it. That's how the Father will be seen for who he is in the Son. I mean it. Whatever you request in this way, I'll do.

Look at the word *ask* in the King James Version. This word in the Greek means, "in my authority or whatever you demand in my rights and privileges, it shall be done for you," or "He will do it." Another translation says he—God—will construct it, create it, make it, fashion it, produce it, or custom-build it. Wow! Authority in his name has the power to get the job done.

3. Believe and depend totally on him. One thing I know for sure is that it would have been wrong for Jesus to ask the disciples, "Why are you so fearful, and why aren't you trusting me?" if he did not expect that his disciples could, in fact, rise up and do what he did, rebuke the storm and tell it to stop. As believers, in order to have faith to speak to our problems in life, we must first develop confidence in Jesus. We must know that he will *never* leave us or forsake us. I like to refer to this as having a revelation that Jesus is *always* in your boat! When you get the revelation that he is with you in anything you go through in life, you know that even if the boat appears to be sinking, it can never go down. You will never drown or be defeated, because Jesus is in your boat. If you think about this in terms of the dispensation of what Grace has provided, you can make the confession, "I can never be defeated because Christ is inside me. The hope of glory!"

So the next time you are faced with a storm in your life, remember these three key things in order to overcome: get in a position of rest, exercise executive authority in his name, and believe and depend totally on him!

Remember, in the beginning of this chapter I shared four throne room realities. God reminded me that I left out one very important reality—Zoe life. So many believers today who have accepted Jesus as their Lord and Savior do not even realize what this really means. From the moment you make this confession, you have access to the Kingdom of God and everything the Kingdom offers! This is a throne room reality that must be understood. When you hear the word throne room, it is indicative of that place in Heaven where God reigns and Jesus is seated at His right hand. The Right hand is symbolic of Gods' throne. Once you accept Jesus as your Lord and Savior, you are part of God's kingdom of his dear Son and you now become seated with Jesus in heavenly places. This seat is a seat of delegated power and authority Jesus gives every believer to operate just like him here on earth! This also means you now have the "life of God," or Zoe, abiding in you! This word *life* in the Greek means "Zoe life," "eternal life," or "the class and life of God" (the God kind of life). Other synonyms include *nature of God, timeless, indestructible, imperishable,* and *life not subject to failure or death.* Zoe is life, disease-killing power living inside every man, woman, boy, or girl who accepts Jesus as their Lord and Savior.

Let's take a look at how God gave us the very Zoe life of Christ, which qualified us to be partakers of Christ's salvation, or Sozo. We said *Sozo* is forgiveness, healing, deliverance, or all the finished works of Jesus. Ephesians 2:5 (KJV) says, "Even when we were dead in sins, he hath quickened us together with Christ, by grace ye are saved." So when we receive salvation, we receive Zoe! As children of God, we need to renew our minds to understand that this was one of the very reasons Jesus was sent by the Father. Look at John 10:10 (KJV): "The thief cometh not, but for to steal, and to kill, and to destroy: I am come that they might have life, and that they might have it more abundantly." This life of abundance that Jesus died for is Zoe. First Peter 1:23 (AMP) says, "for you have been born again [that is, reborn from above—spiritually transformed, renewed, and set apart for His purpose] not of seed which is perishable but [from that which is] imperishable and immortal, that is, through the living and everlasting word of God." This version says that we are reborn from above, from a seed that is imperishable and immortal. This means that inside every believer, the Spirit lives forever—never dying, eternal, everlasting, and indestructible, with permanent life abiding. The indestructible living seed of the Word of God conceives resurrection life within you. This life is equal to its source, God. This life remains the same and is not received because of your self-efforts or works of the flesh. It is a gift from God through the finished works of Christ. In other words, it is a Grace gift. Can you imagine allowing this Zoe life to become a throne room reality for you? No matter what you face on this earth, no matter what impossible task is in front of you, it doesn't move you to doubt, fear, or worry because you have a revelation that you are a part of the God class. Therefore, you operate just like he does.

My friend, I know this seems hard to comprehend, but Jesus explains why there should be a difference in the way we believe we receive the things of God. Under the old covenant, or pre-cross, you had to earn the blessings of God through performance or the works of the law. But post-cross, after the finished works of Jesus, your only requirement is to believe. Let's look at what Jesus says about believing for eternal life in John 3:16 (KJV): "For God so loved the world, that he gave his only begotten Son, that whosoever believeth in him should not perish, but have everlasting life." This scripture tells us that the moment we believe, eternal (everlasting) life comes inside us.

What is a benefit of Zoe life? Zoe life releases divine health. Healing is "the children's bread." (Matthew 15:16 KJV). In other words, it belongs to the child of God. This means if you are under attack in this present moment or sometime in the future with any type of sickness or disease, you have a right as a believer to be totally healed. First Peter 2:24 (KJV) says, "By

His stripes we were healed." That means over two thousand years ago, when Jesus declared on the cross, "It is finished," our healing was purchased by his shed blood. Even though this is an awesome benefit as a believer, it is still not God's best. You see, healing is one thing, but divine health is another. Divine health means walking healthy and whole daily. Zoe, eternal life, is, as I stated earlier, a disease-killing power. That means any sickness, germ, or virus that touches your body as a believer dies instantly in the name of Jesus. You must believe that Zoe, eternal life, is at work in your body. Let me prove this to you by the Word. Romans 8:11 (KJV) says, "But if the Spirit of him that raised up Jesus from the dead dwell in you, he that raised up Christ from the dead shall also quicken your mortal bodies by his Spirit that dwelleth in you." The Amplified translation says this instead of "quicken": "restore to life your mortal (short-lived, perishable) bodies through His Spirit Who dwells in you." Wow! This means that the moment the Spirit of God came into us, he brought life as well (the God kind of life), and that life "quickens," or makes our mortal bodies alive and keeps us walking in divine health. What an awesome throne room reality to meditate on. We are a part of the God class, and therefore, Zoe, eternal life, lives inside us. It is the disease-killing power of God that causes every believer to walk in divine health.

Chapter 5

Arriving at Your Final Place of Rest

Hebrews 11:1 (KJV)

Ephesians 1:3

Ephesians 2:8

Romans 5:1–3

Meditational Scriptures

We all have heard that someone is at his or her final place of rest in the Lord. No more suffering. No more pain. *Rest* is defined as "to cease from work or movement, in order to relax, refresh oneself, or recover strength." (Merriam-Webster, 2019). So why, as believers, do we feel that the only rest is when we die and go home to be with the Lord? Jesus said he came that we might have life and have it more abundantly. The abundant life he was referring to was to be experienced here on earth.

In the beginning of this book, I began by explaining Grace. Grace is God's unmerited favor, goodness, and love all in the form of his Son, Jesus. I explained the law, which was under the old covenant and how, because of the "better or new covenant," Jesus Christ, we are no longer subject to the law but are in the dispensation of Grace. All promises we find in God's Word belong to us as believers, and we do not work to receive them; Jesus already did the work on the cross. We must simply believe! Our beliefs, total trust, and dependence on God and his Word, and the knowledge of the finished works of his Son, Jesus, on the cross all help us to arrive at our final places of rest here on earth. Rest carries us through any situation or circumstance we are faced with.

In this chapter, I share what I now believe is the highest form of faith—rest. I also share how to arrive at this place of total trust and dependence on God and his Word. Hopefully from the previous chapters, you now have a total understanding of Grace. Grace makes everything available to us as believers through the finished works of Jesus on the cross. Faith in what Grace has already provided now takes by faith what Grace makes!

Hebrews 11:1 (KJV) begins by telling us faith is the substance of things hoped for. Faith is now, in the present. When you get a full revelation of *now* faith, you find rest and know that you are positioned in a place of belief, trust, and dependence on Jesus! Not people, pastors, bishops, deacons but our faith. Our beliefs are solely on Jesus. "Now" is defined as "at the present time or moment." When you have faith, you believe that you already received what you believed in the present time or moment needed.

How can you rest and have this faith? Through the finished works of Christ. Everything we need is found in him. He has already made provision on the cross for everything. Jesus provided health for sickness,wealth for poverty, and life for death. So think about Grace (God's undeserved favor and goodness), his love, which is his Son! Grace is a person, and his name is Jesus. When we get a revelation of his love and his desire to provide whatever we need, we then go into a daily position of rest. There is no deep secret. It is a decision based on our trust. Everything is already done and ours, but we must have the right mind-set. Ephesians 2:8 (KJV) confirms Grace makes and faith takes: "For by Grace are you saved through faith." This word "saved" is Sozo—forgiven, healed, delivered, prospered, whole, all the finished works.

So he provided it, but we must release our faith to receive what he already provided. To receive is to take delivery of or accept something given, presented, sent, or communicated. Ask yourself, "Have I really received this gift of Grace?" Have you released your faith? To release something is to allow it or make it to escape from confinement, move, act, and flow freely; in other words, to remove restrictions so that it becomes available. What is keeping you from releasing your faith in what Grace has already provided? Before you will ever find your final destination of rest, you must release your faith to believe that you can even have what you need or be set free from your circumstance or situation. Jesus provided everything we need, but if we do not release our faith, we will not see it. Faith is a positive response to the Word and what Jesus has already done. You believe, receive, and act on it. It is a verbal or physical reaction to what Grace has done. Have you declared something that does not make sense in the natural? God has already provided, but are we declaring? Abraham did not see he had a son. He just believed when he responded, and told everyone his name was what God declared it was, Abraham, though his name was originally Abram. Abraham is known as the "Father of Faith." He is a great example of what faith looks like and does. It believes only! Abraham remained in faith and took no thought by saying. What does that mean? Remain in faith and do not listen to bad news, people talking, the devil saying what you will not have, and so on. You cannot speak doubt. This is what I am referring to when I said Abraham remained in faith and took no though by saying. When you stop listening to anything contrary to the Word of God, you are in faith. You refuse to speak anything negative that does not line up to what God has already said in his word! Rebuke, cast out, and do not pay attention to and negative thoughts that come in your mind, or people speak out loud. Just keep believing!

Everything is a spiritual blessing before it is a natural one. "God has blessed us with all spiritual blessings in heavenly places (the spirit realm)." (Ephesians 1:3 KJV). They are spiritual blessings because they came through the shed blood of Jesus. It takes the believer saying and doing something, not works like the law required, but by exercising his or her faith.

In the natural, it does not make sense when, for example,

you believe in getting a new car, hang a picture of keys, and give thanks in advance for the car. Doing this does not make sense, but it does make faith. The Lord told me I want to do so much for believers, but they will not step out in faith and give a physical or verbal action. For instance, let's say a person says, "I need new clothes." That person should clean out a section in the closet and begin every day by saying, "This is where my new clothes will go." The person gives physical and verbal expressions of faith. He or she asks the Holy Spirit to reveal to him or her what needs to be done as a physical and verbal expression of faith for what he or she is believing.

Say and do something. Grace has already provided it, but the Word says that without faith, it is impossible to please God. So you will not see it until you have faith for it. I heard the Lord say, "Go to the ATM, and print out your total balance. If it is not what you want, draw a line through it, and write what you want it to be. Place it beside your bed, and every time you wake up, point to it and say, 'Lord, I thank you that this is my bank account amount. I believe I receive it.'" You are keeping your faith in the field. This is something I like to refer to when I have found a scripture to cover my case and begin to plant the seed in my heart by meditating on God's Word. Just like the farmer plants the seed in his field and waters and takes care of the seed, you keep the seed, or Word of God, in your field, which is your heart, where you hide the Word of God you are believing. We have to do something to cause what he has already provided to manifest. Think of something you know you cannot do, and trust God to do it in this season. He is a God of the impossible! Faith opens the door for the blessings God has already provided, and our faith will take hold of them!

Faith goes beyond reason. Romans 5:1 (KJV) says, "Therefore being justified by faith we have peace with God through our Lord Jesus Christ." We are declared righteous through our faith in Jesus. We have right standing with God, so the blessings are supposed to come to the believer who is justified through faith in him. It does not matter what you have ever done. Nothing can cancel your justification, not even mistakes. The blood of Jesus has forgiven past, present, and future sins. We are righteous not based on performance but on what Jesus did. We are supposed to do right and strive for perfection, but we are not perfect. That is why we have a perfect Savior. Jesus and his blood justifies us, and gives us right standing with God, not our works. Remember that under the law, we had to do or perform to receive. But under Grace, we just believe and receive. I love the gospel or the good news of Jesus (Grace) because it is foolproof. We cannot mess it up. We do not live under a confession economy; we live under a new dispensation of a blood economy. And if we believe in him, we are justified by faith, not works through the shed blood of Jesus. Grace is not a license to sin. It makes you feel and love Jesus more. When you get a revelation of Grace and his love, it makes you fall in love with Jesus and not want to sin. Revelation of Grace causes your nature to change. Even in the midst of doing wrong, you will not want to do it. You will do your best to live for Jesus, whom you love.

Go back and look at Romans 5:2–4 in the Amplified version:

> Through Him also we have [our] access (entrance, introduction) by faith into this grace (state of God's favor) in which we [firmly and safely] stand. And let us rejoice and exult in our hope of experiencing and enjoying the glory of God. Moreover [let us also be full of joy now!] let us exult and triumph in our troubles and rejoice in our sufferings, knowing that pressure and affliction and hardship produce patient *and* unswerving endurance. And endurance (fortitude) develops maturity of [c]character (approved faith and [d]tried integrity). And character [of this sort] produces [the habit of] [e]joyful and confident hope of eternal salvation.

71

This scripture says that we have access to the Grace of God by faith. So again, Grace makes and faith takes. Whatever Grace or God has done through Jesus to make the promise possible, our faith must take hold of the promise by a response, which is a verbal or physical action.

We must simply believe God's Word! This is what believing looks like in the natural. When you believe, trust, lean on, and depend on Jesus, there will be action, or a "faith response," to what you believe. Get this: Your faith response is not to get God to do something that he has already done through the finished works of Jesus. Your faith response is to position yourself to receive what God has already done by Grace. Faith is resting. The body of Christ can learn a valuable lesson from the children of Israel and the importance of entering into God's final place of rest. We see in Hebrews 3:16–19 (KJV) what happens when we do not rest: "For some, when they had heard, did provoke: howbeit not all that came out of Egypt by Moses. But with whom was he grieved forty years? Was it not with them that had sinned, whose carcases fell in the wilderness? And to whom sware he that they should not enter into his rest, but to them that believed not?"

So we see that the children of Israel could not enter in because of unbelief. This scripture shows that even though God loved the children of Israel, not trusting and resting in what he promised them hindered them from entering the Promised Land, which was flowing with milk and honey. Everyone over age twenty died in the wilderness and never got a chance to enjoy the blessings. However, everyone twenty years old and younger was allowed to enter, along with Joshua and Caleb. Why were Joshua and Caleb allowed to enter in since they were over twenty years of age? These men declared that in spite of what appeared to be giants in the land, they were confident that with God, they were well able to overcome these giants. Sometimes, because of your age, God overlooks ignorance to the Word, which was the case for those under twenty years of age. God is also looking for someone to simply believe, like Joshua and Caleb, whom he elevated to the next level. The children of Israel's unwillingness to adhere to, trust in, and rely on God put them in a state of unbelief. What is keeping you from resting? What promises are you not receiving because of your unbelief and inability to rest in what God says? Joshua and Caleb had another spirit or attitude. It was a spirit of faith, resting in what God already provided. Get this: even God rested! The body of Christ needs to understand that coming to a final place of rest is a God ideal that he wants his children to follow.

Look at Hebrews 4:2–4 (KJV). It says, "For unto us was the

gospel preached, as well as unto them: but the word preached did not profit them, not being mixed with faith in them that heard it. For we which have believed do enter into rest, as he said, As I have sworn in my wrath, if they shall enter into my rest: although the works were finished from the foundation of the world. For he spake in a certain place of the seventh day on this wise, And God did rest the seventh day from all his works."

The gospel is the nearly too good to be true news, and when it comes, you have to mix faith with what you hear. Remember, a response is a viral or physical reaction. Have you said or done something once you have heard the Word? In the scripture above, we are reminded that the works were finished before the foundation of the world. God made the world in six days, and when it was finished, he rested. He did not rest because he was tired. He rested because it was finished. God gave the earth to humankind after everything was already provided to live and be successful. Once this was finished, he made Adam and Eve. When Jesus went to the cross, he said, "It is finished!" What he was telling us now as believers was to rest in his finished works because everything that we would ever need in life and godliness was being given to us because of his shedding of blood on the cross. So if we are truly resting, we are reminding ourselves to cease from our own works or performances by trying to do something we think will make God move on our behalf. Stop trying to pray long hours to get God to respond; stop trying to live holy just because you think God will accept you. He has already accepted you. Your acceptance is not based on your attempt to live holy. Because of Grace, you should desire to live holy. Everything is already finished, already done. Your part now is to *believe*. When you simply start believing in Jesus and what Grace has already provided through the blood of Jesus, you will begin to rest. I understand that it is not easy; it requires something. The Word says in Hebrews 4:9–11 (KJV) that we labor to rest: "Here remaineth therefore a rest to the people of God. "For he that is entered into his rest, he also hath ceased from his own works, as God did from his. Let us labour therefore to enter into that rest, lest any man fall after the same example of unbelief."

This scripture tells us that God is still waiting on his people to enter into his rest. There is a difference between the world's rest and his rest. The world defines rests as inactivity or not doing anything but sleeping. God defines rest as having complete confidence in the finished works of Jesus, which allows you to cease from your own work or performance. Sometimes, this requires us to get into a position of victory. Our five senses will fight us in our minds, wills, and emotions. We will begin to think that what we are believing in God for may never happen. Laboring to rest is fighting with everything within you to get yourself to a place of peace and confidence. You then confess the Word on the situation you are going through. You begin meditating on the Word, which is to mutter it, say it over and over again, look at, and think on it repeatedly until it gets inside you and creates an image of what you are believing for. When you do this, trouble can be all around you, but it will not be able to move you from your stand. This is what laboring looks like, doing whatever you are led to do to get you to a final place of rest.

I also recommend praise. The scripture says to the believer that for the spirit of heaviness, release the garment of praise. Praise takes your focus off of yourself and the problem and places it on Jesus. When you place your mind on Jesus, you place it on what he has already provided, and it causes you to stay seated in heavenly places in Christ Jesus! You now begin to rest your mind from worrying about what is going on. I think this is what the writer was trying to explain in Hebrews 4:12 (AMP):

> Let us therefore make every effort to enter that rest
> [of God, to know and experience it for ourselves],
> so that no one will fall by following the same
> example of disobedience [as those who died in

the wilderness]. For the word of God is living and active and full of power [making it operative, energizing, and effective]. It is sharper than any two-edged [a]sword, penetrating as far as the division of the [b]soul and spirit [the completeness of a person], and of both joints and marrow [the deepest parts of our nature], exposing *and* judging the very thoughts and intentions of the heart.

Wow, the Word of God will work powerfully to put you in a place of rest. It is always building you up on the inside, operating and penetrating even your soul, which is your mind, will, and emotions. The Word itself will usher you into a place of rest. Glory!

Finally, I want to share ten keys I believe will be just what you need to get yourself to a final place of rest. Each key encourages you to rest in Jesus and causes you to receive what the blood of Jesus has already provided for you. These keys are a road map to experiencing successful outcomes. I refer to these keys as the Holy Ghost GPS system. Your GPS system in your car works every time; it never fails to get you to your destination. That is the natural. God's spiritual GPS system is more powerful than that.

Let's examine these ten keys.

1. You must realize you are already blessed with all spiritual blessings. Ephesians 1:3 (KJV) says, "Blessed be the God and Father of our Lord Jesus Christ, who hath blessed us with all spiritual blessings in heavenly places in Christ." This scripture indicates that the tense of what you are believing is important. He "*hath* blessed us" indicates everything is already done and in heavenly places or the realm of the spirit for those who are seated in Christ Jesus. When we stay seated, we remain in a place of rest or faith in the finished works.

2. You must understand that faith takes what Grace makes. Ephesians 2:8–9 (KJV) says, "For by grace are ye saved through faith; and that not of yourselves: it is the gift of God: Not of works, lest any man should boast." Grace is unmerited favor, but faith is a positive response of Grace. Both need each other and can't work without the other. Being saved by Grace means salvation. Remember, the Greek meaning for salvation is Sozo, which not only means born again but forgiveness, healing, deliverance, soundness, safety, protection, preservation, prosperity, wholeness, and all the finished works of Jesus. Grace

has already provided Sozo, but faith must be released in order to obtain these blessings.

3. You must make a decision to rest in the finished work of Jesus. John 19:30 (KJV) says, "When Jesus therefore had received the vinegar, he said, It is finished: and he bowed his head, and gave up the ghost." When Jesus declared it is finished, he was saying to all the world what Satan had done was destroyed and broken off of humanity. Believe in me, trust in me, depend on me, and you will always have victory in me.

4. You must labor to rest. Hebrews 4:11 (KJV) says, "For he that is entered into his rest, he also hath ceased from his own works, as God did from his. Let us labour therefore to enter into that rest, lest any man fall after the same example of unbelief." Keep reminding yourself this scripture says labor to rest, not labor to be healed or to get God to do something new. No, it says labor to rest, to get yourself in position to have confidence and total dependence on what Jesus and his blood has already provided.

5. You must believe God loves you. 1 John 4:19 (KJV) says, "We love him, because he first loved us." Under the new covenant of Grace, it is not how you love God but how

you must believe in his love for you. When you get a revelation of how much he loves you, when you are sick, you know he will heal you. If you are bound, you know he will deliver you. When you are in trouble, you know without a doubt he will bring you out and never leave you or forsake you. That is why the Bible says "faith worketh by love,"(Galatians 5:6 KJV), not how much you love God, but how much he loves you!

6. You must understand the Holy Spirit will lead you into all truth, not the law. Romans 7:5–6 (KJV) says, "For when we were in the flesh, the motions of sins, which were by the law, did work in our members to bring forth fruit unto death. But now we are delivered from the law, that being dead wherein we were held; that we should serve in newness of spirit, and not in the oldness of the letter." Now look at this same scripture in the Amplified version: "When we were living in the flesh [trapped by sin], the sinful passions, which were awakened by [that which] the Law [identifies as sin], were at work in our body to bear fruit for death [since the willingness to sin led to death and separation from God]. But now we have been released from the Law and its penalty, having died [through Christ] to that by which we were held

captive, so that we serve [God] in the newness of the Spirit and not in the oldness of the letter [of the Law]." The law under the old covenant brought people to guilt, condemnation, and to the end of themselves, crying out, "I need a Savior." Grace in the new covenant, not the law, allows the Holy Spirit to guide you and convict you through a personal relationship with him. Yes, him. The Holy Spirit is a person, not a thing. You will begin to sense promptings or leadings to walk before God as a new creation in Christ.

7. You must make confessions motivated by what you believe. 2 Corinthians 4:13 (KJV) says, "We having the same spirit of faith, according as it is written, I believed, and therefore have I spoken; we also believe, and therefore speak." Confessions are powerful. They are defined in the Greek as "to agree and say the same thing." Understand, however, confessing is not just thinking, *If I say it enough, I can make it happen.* That is the wrong mind-set. You must believe in your heart and then release your faith, which makes confessions effective.

8. You must develop a lifestyle of worship and praise. 1 Thessalonians 5:18 (KJV) says, "In every thing give thanks: for this is the will of God in Christ Jesus

concerning you." Notice this says *in* everything, not *for* everything. In other words, right in the middle of your trouble or your difficulties of life, break out worship and praise. You worship him for who he is. You praise him for what he's already done.

9. Take authority over every negative thought. 2 Corinthians10:4–5 (KJV) says, "For the weapons of our warfare are not carnal, but mighty through God to the pulling down of strong holds; Casting down imaginations, and every high thing that exalteth itself against the knowledge of God, and bringing into captivity every thought to the obedience of Christ." This means casting down every negative thought, dream, suggestion, or feeling that does not line up with the Word, bringing them into captivity or the obedience of Christ and his Word. This is how you stop strongholds of negativity from taking root in your mind. Have you heard the phrase, "The mind is a terrible thing to waste"? Well, why do you allow the enemy to rent space in your mind? The battlefield of the mind determines whether you experience victory in your life. Every person's mind has two parts, the conscious and subconscious. The conscious mind is your thinker, chooser, the intellect, and the five

senses. The subconscious is your emotional mind-set. It is what has been downloaded, and it remains in your subconscious. It is where all your habits are formed and where your belief system abides. So if you have thoughts of unbelief or negativity, they become a paradigm that must now be reprogrammed with the Word of God by repetition and meditation. We understand how important this reprogramming of old paradigms is when we read the scripture that says, "as a man thinketh in his heart, so is he." (Proverbs 23:7).

10. You must only believe and depend on Jesus. Galatians 2:21 (KJV) says, "I do not frustrate the grace of God: for if righteousness come by the law, then Christ is dead in vain." Now look at this same scripture in the New Living Translation version for more clarity: "I do not treat the grace of God as meaningless. For if keeping the law could make us right with God, then there was no need for Christ to die." This last key is so important because our faith must always be in Jesus, *not* our works. Religion will always require performance or self-effort to earn a relationship with and to receive the blessings of God. Our total trust must be in Jesus Christ, knowing that it is only because of him we have righteousness or

right standing. We are now able to stand right in the presence of God without guilt or shame and get our prayers answered. When you get this revelation of faith and begin operating in it daily, you will find your true rest. Faith is the highest form of rest. So I declare, only believe, only trust, and rest in the finished works of Jesus Christ!

Chapter 6

Faith Responses and Confessions That Bring Rest

My friend, this book was written to build confidence and trust in Jesus and his finished works. Under the law, he was a judge of sins. But under Grace, he is a Father. Never again should you doubt, worry, or fear that what God promised in his Word will not come to pass. The moment Jesus said, "It is finished" on the cross, his blood purchased our freedom to have victory in every area of life. Even when we may sin or miss the mark, we should repent and not allow the enemy to ever keep us in condemnation. Why? Because we are "sealed unto the day of redemption." This means no matter what you face in life, Grace has you covered.

When you make the decision to only believe in and depend on Jesus and his finished works, you will live in a state of victory and experience successful outcomes. Following are some confessions I believe will help you experience successful outcomes. Confess these positive faith responses daily to renew your faith in the finished works of Christ. In doing so, you will no doubt reach a place of rest, which is the highest form of faith!

Daily Faith Responses

Scripture Verse

Blessed be the God and Father of our Lord Jesus Christ, who hath blessed us with all spiritual blessings in heavenly places in Christ. (Ephesians 1:3 KJV)

Faith Response

In the name of Jesus, every spiritual blessing in heaven belongs to me. Therefore, I am blessed with all spiritual blessings in heavenly places in Christ Jesus.

Now pray in the Spirit at least five minutes.

Scripture Verse

According as he hath chosen us in him before the foundation of the world, that we should be holy and without blame before him in love. (Ephesians 1:4 KJV)

Faith Response

In Christ I am holy and blameless, according as he has chosen me before the foundation of the world. I am set apart for God, and I am no longer condemned.

Now pray in the Spirit for at least five minutes.

Scripture Verse

Having predestinated us unto the adoption of children by Jesus Christ to himself, according to the good pleasure of his will. (Ephesians 1:5 KJV)

Faith Response

In Christ, I am predestined unto sonship. I've been adopted as an heir, and now I have the life and nature of God in my human flesh.

Scripture Reference

To the praise of the glory of his grace, wherein he hath made us accepted in the beloved. (Ephesians 1:6 KJV)

Faith Response

In Christ I am accepted in the beloved, which means I am endued with special divine favor and honor.

Now pray in the Spirit at least five minutes.

Scripture Verse

In whom we have redemption through his blood, the forgiveness of sins, according to the riches of his grace. (Ephesians 1:7 KJV)

Faith Response

In Christ I have redemption through his blood, which means I've been taken out of the control and dominion of the devil in Jesus's name. In Christ I am forgiven of all my sins. I have remission of sins, a total removal and blotting out. Yes, when he shed his blood and died on the cross, he forgave me of past, present, and future sins in Jesus's name.

Now pray in the Spirit at least five minutes.

Scripture Verse

In whom also we have obtained an inheritance, being predestinated according to the purpose of him who worketh all things after the counsel of his own will. (Ephesians 1:11 KJV)

Faith Response

I have obtained an inheritance in Christ Jesus. I am poor no more. I have a spiritual and legal right to every blessing in the finished work of Jesus.

Now pray in the Spirit at least five minutes.

Scripture Verse

In whom ye also trusted, after that ye heard the word of truth, the gospel of your salvation. (Ephesians 1:13 KJV)

Faith Response

In Christ I have the gospel of salvation. Yes, because Jesus is my Lord and Savior, I have forgiveness, healing, deliverance, soundness, safety, protection, preservation, prosperity, wholeness, and all the finished works of Jesus.

Now pray in the Spirit at least five minutes.

Scripture Verse

in whom also after that ye believed, ye were sealed with that holy Spirit of promise. (Ephesians 1:13 KJV)

Faith Response

In Christ I am sealed with the Holy Spirit of promise unto the day of redemption; he will never leave me or forsake me. He lives in me eternally.

Now pray in the Spirit at least five minutes.

Scripture Reference

That the God of our Lord Jesus Christ, the Father of glory, may give unto you the spirit of wisdom and revelation in the knowledge of him. (Ephesians 1:17 KJV)

Faith Response

In Christ I have the spirit of wisdom and revelation in the knowledge of him. I have insight into mysteries and secrets in the intimate knowledge of him.

Now pray in the Spirit at least five minutes.

Scripture Verse

The eyes of your understanding being enlightened; that ye may know what is the hope of his calling, and what the riches of the glory of his inheritance in the saints. (Ephesians 1:18 KJV)

Faith Response

In Christ the eyes of my understanding are enlightened, the eyes of my heart are filled with light, and I understand the hope to which he's called me and his glorious inheritance. (Ephesians 1:18 KJV)

Now pray in the Spirit at least five minutes.

—————————

Scripture Verse

And what is the exceeding greatness of his power to us-ward who believe, according to the working of his mighty power. (Ephesians 1:19 KJV)

Faith Response

In Christ I have the exceeding greatness of his power in me. The immeasurable, unlimited, surpassing ability of God is working in me and working for me. It is the same Dunamis power and might that raised Jesus from the dead.

Now pray in the Spirit at least five minutes.

Resting in the Power of His Executive Authority Daily Confession

Father, in the name of Jesus, I thank you that you have made me to be seated in heavenly places in Christ Jesus.

Therefore, for every problem, circumstance, or situation that happens in my life or in the lives of my loved ones, I have the executive power and authority of Jesus Christ of Nazareth to speak to the problem, speak to the circumstance, speak to the situation, and it must obey me and be in subjection to the word I speak. I speak from a place of victory and never defeat!

Thank you, Lord, that everything I need, every spiritual blessing, is in heavenly places, in Christ Jesus. Every time I maintain a position of rest in him, rest in his Word, and rest in his victory over the enemy, spiritual blessings are released from heavenly places into my life and the lives of everyone I pray for!

Lord, I make a decision now to exercise daily my executive power and authority you have given me and rest in Christ Jesus always. I give thanks in advance for the victory in every area of my life and my loved ones' lives in Jesus's name!

I function from a place of glory, power, authority, and dominion, separated from the debilitating effects of sin, corruption, and darkness in Jesus's name. Amen.

Printed in the United States
By Bookmasters